Flying by the Seat of Your Pants

More Absurdities and Realities of Special Education

Cartoons by Michael F. Giangreco

Illustrations by Kevin Ruelle

Peytral Publications, Inc.
Minnetonka, MN 55345
952-949-8707

Publisher's Cataloguing-in-Publication
(Provided by Quality Books, Inc.)

Giangreco, Michael F., 1956-
    Flying by the seat of your pants : more absurdities and realities of special education / cartoons by Michael F. Giangreco ; illustrations by Kevin Ruelle. -- 1st ed.
        p. cm.
    ISBN: 1-890455-41-5

    1. Special education--United States--Humor.
    2. Mainstreaming in education--United States--Humor.
    3. Handicapped children--Education--United States--Humor.
    4. Home and school--United States--Humor. I. Ruelle, Kevin.
    II. Title.

    LA23.G532 1999   371.9'0207
                                       QBI98-1338

        LCCN: 98-067964

Cartoon illustrations by Kevin Ruelle
Printed in the United States of America

Peytral Publications, Inc.
PO Box 1162
Minnetonka, MN 55345
(952) 949-8707
www.peytral.com

Contents

About the Author

Michael F. Giangreco, Ph.D., is a Research Associate Professor at the University of Vermont (UVM). His work as a faculty member at UVM since 1988 has been on various projects with colleagues at the Center on Disability and Community Inclusion (the University Affiliated Program of Vermont) in the College of Education and Social Services. Since 1975 he has worked with children and adults with and without disabilities in a variety of capacities including camp counselor, community residence counselor, special education teacher, special education coordinator, educational consultant, university teacher, and researcher. Since 1982 he has written a number of traditional research studies, book chapters, and books. In 1998 Michael had his first book of cartoons published (Ants in His Pants: Absurdities and Realities of Special Education). Although he will continue his more traditional writing, he plans to continue to infuse humor into his work and find creative ways to share information about the serious issues facing people with disabilities, their families, teachers, and service providers.

About the Illustrator

Kevin Ruelle has been an illustrator in Vermont for twenty years. Cartoons are just one of the many applications of illustration that Kevin uses in his work. He runs a successful commercial art business, Ruelle Design and Illustration, located in Williston, Vermont. He and his associates produce all forms of visual communication and multimedia projects. Kevin lives with his wife, Neidi, and their four children in West Bolton, Vermont.

A Word from the Author

This book of 105 cartoons, Flying by the Seat of Your Pants: More Absurdities and Realities of Special Education, is the second collaborative effort between myself and Kevin Ruelle. The first book, Ants in His Pants: Absurdities and Realities of Special Education, was enthusiastically received by many parents whose children have disabilities and by special educators, classroom teachers, related services providers, and administrators. Given the positive response, we decided to keep going until we had another set to share.

Just like the earlier book, I spent many evenings and late nights creating the original cartoons by generating ideas, making crude sketches, and writing the text. Luckily for you, you will not be subjected to viewing my original drawings (they were pretty bad); that is where Kevin's talents came in. He took the originals and transformed them into the characters and scenes you see in this book. As with the first set of cartoons, this was a synergistic and thoroughly enjoyable experience as the cartoons evolved into their final states.

Knowing that some of you will not have seen the early set of cartoons (Ants in His Pants ...), I decided to repeat some of what I wrote before to ensure that readers have a clear understanding of my underlying thoughts and values in developing these cartoons. First, I value humor and think it is vital to our health, well-being, and creativity. Humor can also be a powerful learning tool. I wanted to address some of the serious issues of special and general education by poking fun at what we (people in the field) do. I have been challenged by the concern that some people might be offended by content that may hit a little too close to home. I have decided to take the chance that people in our field have a sufficient sense of humor to reflect on the satirical aspects of these cartoons, see the humor in them, and use them to promote better schooling. Friends and colleagues have warned me that my cartoons could be misused to promote practices that are the antithesis of what I have worked for my entire professional career. Just so there is no misunderstanding about what these cartoons stand for, I have listed here some of my beliefs related to the cartoon content.

- Individuals with disabilities are still woefully undervalued in our society.

- We waste too many of our resources testing, sorting, and labeling people, usually so we can justify serving, separating, or excluding them.

- The general education classroom (with individually appropriate supports) should be the first placement option for children with disabilities; separate special education schools and classes continue to be unnecessarily overused.

- Inclusive education is desirable; therefore, our efforts should be geared toward finding ways that it can work effectively for increasing numbers of students.

- People of all ages, with and without disabilities, have much to learn from each other.

- Collaborative teamwork is an important element of quality education.

- Families are the cornerstone of ongoing educational planning.

- Establishing a partnership between families and school personnel is vital to quality education.

- Families and professionals should work together to increase effective consumerism by families regarding educational services.

- Competent general educators can effectively teach students with disabilities when provided with appropriate supports.

- Special educators and related service providers (e.g., physical therapists, occupational therapists, speech/language pathologists, school psychologists) can, and do, make important contributions for many students with special educational needs.

- Paraprofessionals are playing an increasingly prominent role in the education of students with disabilities. These hard-working folks typically are underpaid, undertrained, and undersupervised. Too often this means that they inappropriately become the de facto teacher for students with the most complex and challenging educational needs.

- All school personnel need to work under conditions that allow them to provide appropriate education for their students (e.g., adequate staff development and inservice education; supportive supervision; reasonable caseload sizes).

- The IEP (Individual Education Plan) can be a powerful and useful tool to facilitate quality education for students with disabilities. Unfortunately, too often it is misused.

- At the heart of quality education is the relationship among the members of the educational community, the quality of the curriculum, and the integrity of the instruction. We must attend to all three components if we hope to assist students in experiencing valued life outcomes.

So as you read the cartoons, keep in mind that they are meant to encourage better educational practices by highlighting various absurdities of some of the current practices. I hope the cartoons stimulate you to think about things differently and that you find creative ways to use them in your own efforts to improve education for children and youth. I also hope that some of these cartoons make you smile and laugh, because we sure can use more of that in education.

Enjoy!

Michael F. Giangreco

Acknowledgments

So many people inspired and encouraged me throughout this project. Thanks to my colleagues, friends, and family around the country who inspired some of these cartoons or provided input or support: Amanda Dana, Rachel Janney, Dennis Kane, Gloria Kishi, Norman Kunc, Beverly Rainforth, Jane Ross-Allen, Emma VanderKlift, and Marilyn Wessels. Special thanks are extended to Morgan Ruelle and Dan Vogelzang for their technical and creative contributions to the development of these cartoons. My greatest encouragement and many helpful suggestions came from my fun and funny family, my wife, Mary Beth Doyle, and my children, Melanie and Dan. I also wish to thank Roberto and Peggy Hammeken of Peytral Publications. When others were unwilling to take a chance on publishing cartoons about special education, they saw the value in them and took the risk.

SEARCH COMMITTEE MEMBERS
RECOGNIZE THAT TO BE EFFECTIVE IN
SCHOOLS IT HELPS TO HAVE A GOOD
SENSE OF HUMOR.

FRED WAS SHOCKED WHEN HE
READ THE SMALL PRINT.

MRS. GREEN RESORTS TO BRINGING A
LIFE-SIZED CARDBOARD REPLICA OF THE
COUNTY'S MOST TENACIOUS ADVOCATE
TO HER CHILD'S IEP MEETING.

EXTENDING THE CONTINUUM: WHERE WILL IT END?!!

STUDENTS WHO MISBEHAVED IN A SPECIAL ED SCHOOL ARE TRANSFERRED TO A MORE RESTRICTIVE PLACEMENT.

ANOTHER ANNOYING TRUE STORY FROM
THE FILES OF THE INCLUSION PATROL.

A TALE OF TWO SCHOOLS.

AFTER YEARS ELUDING STUDENTS WITH
DISABILITIES, ONE FINALLY CATCHES UP
WITH MRS. SNIPPETT.

MRS. HART GETS PUMPED UP ABOUT
TEACHING A FULL RANGE OF STUDENTS,
BECAUSE EVEN THOUGH IT'S HARD WORK,
THE RESULTS REALLY SHOW.

INCLUSION MISHAP #13:
MRS. SNIPPETT DECIDES IT'S FINALLY TIME TO HAVE HER HEARING TESTED.

MRS. V. IS THE KIND OF CLASSROOM
TEACHER WHO BENDS OVER BACKWARDS
FOR ALL OF HER STUDENTS.

MRS. KING SPORTS HER
WORN SOFTBALL CAP AS A REMINDER
THAT INDIVIDUALIZING TO MEET
UNIQUE STUDENT NEEDS IS
OLD HAT TO GOOD TEACHERS.

PURPOSEFUL
EDUCATIONAL
ACCOMMODATIONS
CREATING
EXCELLENCE

CLUB MEMBERS PREPARE TO READ "EVERYTHING YOU ALWAYS WANTED TO KNOW ABOUT SPECIAL EDUCATION, BUT WERE AFRAID TO ASK."

HELL-BENT ON HELPING

DESPERATE PARENTS RESORT TO
ESTABLISHING THEIR OWN
"FREQUENT INCLUDER PROGRAM."

LUNACY!?

AFTER SEVERAL BAD EXPERIENCES WITH THE LUNAR CYCLE, SCHOOL OFFICIALS DECIDE NOT TO HOLD ANY MORE MEETINGS DURING THE FULL MOON.

IF A STUDENT WITH A DISABILITY FALLS IN THE WOODS, ON THE GROUNDS OF A SPECIAL EDUCATION SCHOOL, AND THERE ARE NO NONDISABLED PEERS THERE TO HEAR HIM, DOES HIS FALL MAKE A SOUND?

THE MOST APPROPRIATE LABEL IS
USUALLY THE ONE PEOPLE'S PARENTS
HAVE GIVEN THEM.

A DISTANT COUSIN OF PINOCCHIO
DISCOVERS HE HAS INHERITED ONE OF
HIS FAMILY'S RECESSIVE TRAITS.

THE EVOLUTION OF SWIMMING LESSONS:
SURPRISINGLY SIMILAR TO THE EVOLUTION
OF INCLUDING STUDENTS WITH
DISABILITIES IN GENERAL EDUCATION.

HARRY CONTINUES HIS EFFORTS
TO GAIN ADMITTANCE TO THE LOCAL
"MOUNTAIN OUT OF A MOLEHILL" SOCIETY.

JOE THINKS A PERISCOPE SHOULD COME AS STANDARD EQUIPMENT WITH EVERY WHEELCHAIR.

EXAMPLES FROM NATURE REMIND US THAT PLACEMENT REALLY DOES MATTER.

AFTER MEETINGS, PHONE CALLS, AND
LETTERS HAD FAILED, ONE PARENT
TRIED A SUBTLE REMINDER.

NOT SO ANCIENT INCLUSIVE PROVERB:
TAKE ACTION!
PERSISTENCE OVERCOMES RESISTANCE.

PEOPLE WITH DISABILITIES DON'T HAVE
ANY SKIN ON THEIR TEETH, AND THEY
SHOULDN'T NEED ANY.

PARENTS FIND NEW WAYS TO RAISE
MONEY FOR EDUCATIONALLY RELATED
LEGAL FEES.

THE THREE MUSKETEERS
OF GOOD PRACTICE:
VALUES, LOGIC, AND RESEARCH
(IN THAT ORDER).

CRAZY LIKE A FOX

PLACING A CHILD WITH A
DISABILITY IN A GENERAL
EDUCATION CLASSROOM IS NOT
ENOUGH TO BE INCLUDED;
IT'S JUST A FOOT IN THE DOOR.

PLACEMENT PROBLEM #32:
FUNCTIONING LEVEL RATHER THAN
CHRONOLOGICAL AGE.

ROY MAKES GOOD ON HIS PROMISE
TO EAT HIS HAT WHEN STUDENTS
WITH SEVERE DISABILITIES ARE
SUCCESSFULLY INCLUDED IN
GENERAL EDUCATION CLASSES.

MEETING MANIA

IN AN EFFORT TO MAINTAIN A
WORKABLE TEAM SIZE, MR. MOODY
SUGGESTS LIMITING MEMBERSHIP TO
THE NUMBER OF PEOPLE THAT
CAN FIT IN A PHONE BOOTH.

MARKING THEIR TERRITORY
TEAM MEMBERS IN EXPERIMENTAL
THERAPY LEARN TO OVERCOME
PRIMITIVE BEHAVIOR.

TEAM MEMBERS FIND FUN WAYS TO
FACILITATE THEIR MEETINGS!

ALAN ALWAYS LOOKS FOR THE
POSITIVE IN EVERY SITUATION.

MISSION IMPOSSIBLE

LARGE CASELOADS FOR
SPECIAL EDUCATORS:
THE NUMBERS JUST DON'T ADD UP!

THE LEAD BALLOONS
OF SPECIAL EDUCATION.

COMMUNICATION BREAKDOWN # 15:
HEARING ANYTHING THROUGH
THE GRAPEVINE CONTINUES TO BE A
VERY UNRELIABLE WAY TO GET
ACCURATE INFORMATION.

COMMUNICATION BREAKDOWN # 21:
FALSE RUMORS ARE SPREAD THAT
MR. MOODY USES ILLEGAL SUBSTANCES.

REDUCING TURNOVER:

EDUCATION OFFICIALS IMPLEMENT PART
OF THEIR EARLY INTERVENTION PROGRAM.

HAVING NEVER ADVANCED PAST
MATH 101 (MATH IN EVERYDAY LIFE),
FRED IS COMFORTED BY THE
REALIZATION THAT HE WAS NOT
ALONE IN HIS FEAR OF FORMULAS.

"FAMILY-CENTERED APPROACHES"
GONE BAD.

HOME PROGRAMMING
COLLIDES WITH
HOME REALITY!

MRS. FOSTER FINDS FASHIONABLE,
FUNCTIONAL FOOTWEAR TO ATTEND HER
DAUGHTER'S DUE PROCESS HEARING.

LOOKING FOR LUCK
IN ALL THE WRONG PLACES.

HELEN HELPS HERSELF HAVE HEALTHIER HABITS.

RECYCLING GONE BAD

SPECIAL EDUCATORS INVENT MISGUIDED
AUTOMATED APPROACHES.

MRS. BAKER EXPERIENCES
"OPTION PARALYSIS."

MAIL ORDER UNIVERSITIES ADD THE
INCREASINGLY POPULAR IEP DIPLOMA TO
THEIR OFFERINGS.

AFTER AN EXHAUSTIVE SEARCH,
MR. MOODY FINDS THE PERFECT TEACHING
ASSISTANT FOR MRS. SNIPPETT.

WHAT CAN HAPPEN WHEN
PARAPROFESSIONALS ARE LEFT TO LEARN
THE ROPES WITHOUT APPROPRIATE
TRAINING AND SUPERVISION.

THE SHADOW KNOWS:

RODNEY'S SUSPICIONS WERE
ACCURATE. UNBEKNOWNST TO HIM,
A PARAPROFESSIONAL HAD BEEN
ASSIGNED TO BE HIS SHADOW.

MR. MOODY CONSIDERS THE
SCHOOL DISTRICT CONSULTANT'S
RECOMMENDATION FOR HIRING AN
INSTRUCTIONAL ASSISTANT WHO WON'T
UNNECESSARILY SHADOW STUDENTS.

TIM NOTICES A MYSTERIOUS FORCE-FIELD
AROUND HIS JOB COACH THAT
CO-WORKERS CANNOT PENETRATE.

CONFUSION REGARDING
"ISTS" AND "OLOGISTS"
STARTS AT AN EARLY AGE.

"WE HAVE WAYS OF MAKING YOU TALK!"

SYLVIA CONTINUALLY STRUGGLES TO
UNDERSTAND THE DIFFERENCES
BETWEEN THE DISCIPLINES.

HAROLD REGRETS NOT ATTENDING THE
INSERVICE ON WHEELCHAIR SAFETY.

PARENTS FINALLY DISCOVER WHY THEIR
CHILDREN SEEM TO HAVE
NEW SUPPORT STAFF EVERY YEAR.

AFTER MONTHS OF PSYCHOTHERAPY, SYLVIA RETRIEVES REPRESSED CHILDHOOD MEMORIES OF THERAPEUTIC POSITIONING THAT EXPLAIN HER SHOE FETISH IN ADULTHOOD.

HALL PATROL

HELEN IS HER NAME,
SAFETY IS HER GAME.

THE DISTRICT'S EXPERIMENTAL METHOD
FOR DETERMINING RELATED SERVICES
WORKS JUST AS WELL AS MAKING THOSE
DECISIONS BEFORE KNOWING A
STUDENT'S IEP GOALS AND OTHER
LEARNING OUTCOMES.

ALL OF THE DISTRICT'S SCHOOL
PSYCHOLOGISTS ARE SUPPLIED WITH
EQUIPMENT TO CARRY OUT THEIR TWO
MOST COMMON FUNCTIONS.

SUPPORT SERVICES THAT ARE
"ONLY AS SPECIAL AS NECESSARY"
FIT JUST RIGHT!

THE INTERSECTION WHERE DIETING
AND REHABILITATION MEET.

IF WE REMODELED BATHROOMS THE WAY
WE DELIVERED SUPPORT SERVICES USING
A SPECIALIST-RELIANT MODEL...

NATURAL SUPPORTS BREATHE;
WHEN USED APPROPRIATELY, THEY MAKE
THINGS FEEL MORE COMFORTABLE.

AFTER TRYING TO FLY BY THE SEAT OF
HIS PANTS, FRED LEARNED THAT GOOD
TEACHING REQUIRES GOOD PLANNING.

STONE-AGE ORIGINS OF SHAPING

ATTEMPTS AT AIRLIFTING CERTAIN
SPECIAL CLASS APPROACHES INTO
REGULAR CLASS ARE UNSUCCESSFUL,
THEY JUST DON'T FIT.

© 1999 MICHAEL F. GIANGRECO. ILLUSTRATION BY KEVIN RUELLE
PEYTRAL PUBLICATIONS, INC. 952-949-8707

GENERATING AND EVALUATING
IDEAS SIMULTANEOUSLY IS LIKE
TRYING TO RIDE A BIKE BY
PEDALING WITH THE BRAKES ON.

STUDENT DATA IS EXTREMELY VALUABLE-
BUT NOT IF IT'S HALF-BAKED.

AFTER A FULL WEEK OF TESTING,
STUDENTS DECIDE TO TURN THE
TABLES AND JUDGE THEIR TEACHERS.

AUTHENTIC ASSESSMENT:
CONSIDER THE ALTERNATIVES.

CARL CHANGES THE "CONDITIONS"
IN HIS OBJECTIVE: "GIVEN A SIDEWALK
ROUTE WITHOUT AN OPEN MANHOLE
COVER, JIM WILL SAFELY WALK FROM
HOME TO WORK..."

TERRORLESS LEARNING

CONSIDERING HER STUDENTS WITHOUT DISABILITIES, MRS. BAKER REALIZES DAVID'S UNUSUAL BEHAVIORS AREN'T THAT UNUSUAL.

AFTER THE SCHOOL DISTRICT
BANNED CORPORAL PUNISHMENT,
STAFF DECIDED ON A NEW MOTTO:
"IF YOU CAN'T BEAT 'EM, JOIN 'EM."

ADJUSTMENT PROBLEMS:
USUALLY THE ADULTS, RARELY THE KIDS.

CONGRESS AUTHORIZES THE ADDITION OF FOUR NEW DISABILITY CATEGORIES TO THE AMERICANS WITH DISABILITIES ACT.

IN AN EFFORT TO CUT THE COSTS OF
SPECIAL EDUCATION, CENTRAL HIGH
SCHOOL PURSUES CORPORATE
SPONSORSHIP FOR EACH OF ITS STAFF.

MRS. SNIPPETT HAD LONG
THOUGHT I.E.P. STOOD FOR
"INCREDIBLY EXCESSIVE PAPERWORK."

AFTER A STRESSFUL MORNING,
PRINCIPAL MOODY IS RELUCTANT TO
RELINQUISH THE ONLY OASIS OF PEACE
AND SOLITUDE HE CAN FIND.

MEDIATION BREAKDOWN #31:
LUCKILY, MR. MOODY'S
MISUNDERSTANDING HELPED HIM FEEL
CALM AND CENTERED.

DUE PROCESS

THE GAME WHERE EVERYBODY GETS A TURN, NOBODY HAS FUN, AND EVEN IF YOU WIN, YOU FEEL LIKE YOU'VE LOST!

BASED ON CURRENT POLITICAL TRENDS, WITHIN TWO DECADES 95% OF THE SCHOOL YEAR WILL BE DEVOTED TO TESTING.

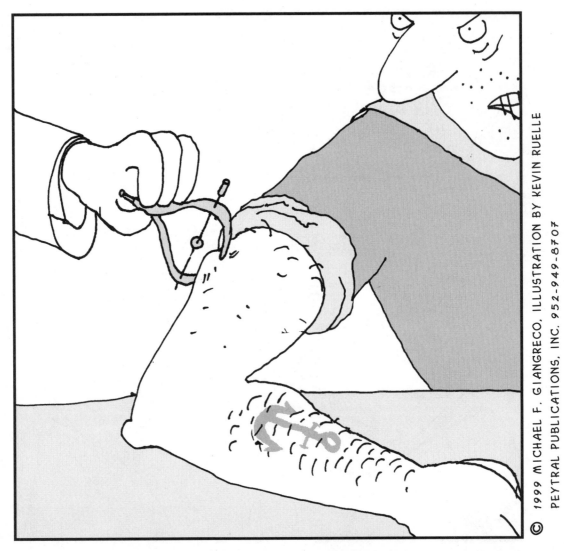

AFTER A SUCCESSFUL INTERVIEW, HARRY UNDERGOES A FINAL SCREENING TO SEE IF HIS SKIN IS THICK ENOUGH TO BE OFFERED AN ADMINISTRATIVE POSITION.

MR. MOODY ESCORTS A DISGRUNTLED
EMPLOYEE TO THE SCHOOL'S NEWLY
ESTABLISHED WHINE CELLAR.

FEW PEOPLE KNOW THAT BEFORE HE WAS
"GENERAL ED" HE WAS "SPECIAL ED."

ED IS DIAGNOSED WITH MULTIPLE
PERSONALITY DISORDER.

NIGHT TERRORS:

STANDARDIZED TESTING STILL HAUNTS HARRY AFTER ALL THESE YEARS.

LITERATURE IN LITERACY
AN ENTIRE GENERATION GREW UP
THINKING DICK, JANE, AND SPOT WERE
SIGNIFICANT LITERARY CHARACTERS.

MR. MOODY LEFT THE DISTRICT
INSERVICE ON TEACHING READING
BEFORE THEY DISCUSSED THE
IMPORTANCE OF COMBINING
LITERATURE AND PHONICS.

CONFUSED BY A STATE EDUCATION DIRECTIVE, MR. MOODY ARRANGES FOR EVERY STUDENT IN HIS SCHOOL TO MEET THE STANDARDS.

MR. MOODY COMPLIES WITH HIS
DISTRICT'S PROMISE TO
MAINTAIN HIGH STANDARDS.

MR. WINKLE'S SECOND GRADE CLASS
SETS A NEW RECORD FOR
SUSTAINED SILENT READING.

STUDENTS CONDUCT A SCIENTIFICALLY
CONTROLLED EXPERIMENT TO VERIFY
THAT TEACHERS REALLY DO HAVE
EYES IN THE BACK OF THEIR HEADS.

WHAT HAPPENS WHEN TEACHERS BECOME
OBSESSED WITH POULTRY PUNS.

MATH ONE-WAY

MATH OUT OF THE WAY

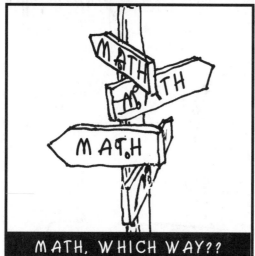

MATH, WHICH WAY??

MATH MY WAY

A POPULAR MATH PROGRAM SPAWNS CHEAP IMITATIONS.

INCLUSIVE EDUCATION:
PROVING YOU CAN DREAM WITH YOUR HEAD IN THE CLOUDS AND STILL HAVE YOUR FEET FIRMLY ON THE GROUND.

Notes

Notes

Notes

Notes

Notes

Notes

Notes

Notes

Notes